# DARKNESS EVERYWHERE

## THE ASSASSINATION OF MOHANDAS GANDHI

MATT DOEDEN

TWENTY-FIRST CENTURY BOOKS / MINNEAPOLIS

## For Mom

Twenty-First Century Books
A division of Lerner Publishing Group, Inc.
241 First Avenue North
Minneapolis, MN 55401 U.S.A.

Website address: www.lernerbooks.com


Library of Congress Cataloging-in-Publication Data

Doeden, Matt.
    Darkness everywhere : the assassination of Mohandas Gandhi / by Matt
Doeden.
      p.  cm.
    Includes bibliographical references and index.
    ISBN 978-0-7613-5483-3 (library binding : alkaline paper)
    ISBN 978-1-4677-1659-8 (eBook)
    1. Gandhi, Mahatma, 1869-1948—Juvenile literature. 2. Statesmen—India—
Biography—Juvenile literature. 3. Nationalists—India—Biography—Juvenile
literature. 4. Pacifists—India—Biography—Juvenile literature. 5. India—Politics
and government—1919-1947—Juvenile literature. I. Title.
DS481.G3D59 2014
954.03'5092—dc23 [B]                      2012041287

Manufactured in the United States of America
1 – BP – 7/15/13

# CONTENTS

# "OUR LIGHT HAS GONE OUT"

> "Gandhi has gone out of our lives and there is darkness everywhere."
>
> —Indian prime minister Jawaharlal Nehru, speaking of Gandhi's assassination in a national radio broadcast, January 30, 1948

On January 31, 1948, the world awoke to a shocking headline. Mohandas Gandhi, the spiritual leader of India and the world's most famous pacifist, was dead. He had been shot and killed the day before at a prayer ceremony in Delhi, India. His assassin was Nathuram Godse, a member of an extremist Hindu nationalist group. In a period of intense Hindu-Muslim tension in India, Godse was angered by what he saw as Gandhi's appeasement of India's Muslim population. He also resented that Gandhi had been unable to prevent India from splitting into two separate nations—India and Pakistan.

On the evening of the assassination, Godse went to the grounds of Birla House in New Delhi, where Gandhi held his daily prayer meetings. He approached Gandhi outside the building, bowed, and shot him three times at point-blank range. Gandhi fell to the ground, his handspun white clothing stained red with blood. His followers rushed him inside and called for his doctor. But it was too late. Gandhi was dead at the age of seventy-eight. Godse did not flee the scene. Instead, the gathered crowd seized his gun, and Godse voluntarily surrendered himself to the police.

Gandhi's death was front-page news around the globe. Many people were shocked. They couldn't believe that the man called Mahatma, or "great soul," was dead. He had led a decades-long resistance to British rule of India, rejecting all forms of violence. Others weren't surprised. After all, another attempt on Gandhi's life had failed just ten days earlier, one of several attempts over the years to kill the Mahatma.

India's prime minister Jawaharlal Nehru—a close friend and political ally of Gandhi's—announced a thirteen-day period of mourning, with flags flown at half-staff. "Gandhi has gone out of our lives and there is darkness everywhere," said Nehru in a radio address to his nation. "The father of our nation is no more—no longer will we run to him for advice and solace. . . . This is a terrible blow to millions and millions in our country. . . . Our light has gone out, but the light that shone in this country was no ordinary light. For a thousand years that light will be seen in this country and the world will see it. . . . Oh that this has happened to us! There was so much more to do."

Many people around the world asked themselves, What would become of India without Gandhi? Violence in India and newly formed Pakistan was escalating. Gandhi had been a powerful voice for peace. The January 31 edition of the *New York Times* commented that with Gandhi's death, India was at a crossroads. Would the newly independent nation follow a road to peace and survive? Or would it collapse under the weight of violence between Hindu and Muslim communities? The answer was unclear. One thing was certain, however. With Gandhi gone, India would never be the same.

## Chapter One
# A LIFE

"We notice [love] between father and son, between brother and sister, friend and friend. But we have to learn to use that force among all that lives, and in the use of it consists our knowledge of God. Where there is love there is life; hatred leads to destruction."

*—Mohandas Gandhi,*
*October 6, 1921*

Mohandas Karamchand Gandhi was born October 2, 1869, in Porbandar, India. His parents were devout followers of the Hindu religion, as were about 80 percent of India's people. Mohandas was the youngest of the couple's three surviving children.

As Hindus the Gandhi family were members of a merchant caste (class of society) called Vaishya. A Hindu's caste traditionally determined a person's place in that society. Membership in the Vaishya caste, for example, would have led Gandhi to live as a merchant or a landowner. But by the time of Gandhi's birth, the rigidity of the caste system had lessened, and he could be almost anything he wanted to be. Gandhi learned at a young age, however, that this flexibility did not extend to a large section of the population known as untouchables. These people were shunned by society and were allowed to do only the lowest, least desirable jobs.

Putlibai *(left)* and Karamchand Gandhi *(right)* raised their children, including Mohandas, in Porbandar, India. This city is in the Indian state of Gujarat and lies on the coast of the Arabian Sea.

# CASTE SYSTEM

The Hindu caste system is thousands of years old. Its impact on social life has diminished in India over the years as a result of modern legislation outlawing discrimination based on caste.

Historically, the caste system has divided Hindus into four basic classes. Untouchables are a separate group of people outside the caste system. A person's caste is determined by birth. Movement into or out of a caste is almost impossible.

**BRAHMIN:** This is the cast of priests, who are closest to the gods. They rank highest in the caste system and are expected to devote their time to spiritual pursuits.

**KSHATRIYA:** This is the warrior class. Members of this caste rank below the Brahmin and are charged with protecting the people and offering sacrifices to the gods.

**VAISHYA:** This is the merchant class and the one to which Gandhi belonged. Members of this caste are charged with conducting trade, farming, and owning land.

**SUDRA:** This is the lowest-ranking caste. It is the caste of common laborers and peasants. At one time in history, the members of this caste were not allowed to study religious texts or to eat in the presence of higher castes.

**UNTOUCHABLE:** Members of this class, also known as Dalits, fall outside the caste system altogether. Historically, the caste was considered impure and unfit to interact with members of any of the four castes. They took on the lowest of jobs and were not allowed to touch a member of a higher class. The Indian government officially outlawed this classification in 1950. But it remains a reality of life for millions of poor Indians in the twenty-first century, many of whom face discrimination because of their social ranking as untouchables.

Gandhi's mother taught him to be devoted to his faith. He was also deeply influenced by ancient Indian faiths, including Jainism and a branch of Hinduism known as Vaishnavism. These religions hold to principles of self-control, humility, and nonviolence. Their teachings made a big impact on Gandhi, shaping both his personality and his worldview.

## A TIMID CHILD

Compared to much of India, which was rife with extreme poverty, the Gandhi family lived well. Karamchand Gandhi was a skilled politician, and so the family had money and status. For the first six years of his life, Mohandas's home was in Porbandar, on the Arabian Sea. When Mohandas was seven years old, his father rose to the rank of diwan, or prime minister, of the city of Rajkot.

Mohandas's parents wanted their son to be educated so that he could one day be a diwan, like his father. The youngster attended school, where he learned to read and write in his native language of Gujarati. (At the time, only a select few Indian children attended school. Most stayed home to help with housework or earned money with jobs outside the home.) While he excelled at his schoolwork, Gandhi lagged behind socially. There was little about him that hinted at future greatness.

"I used to be shy and avoided all company," he later said. "My books and my lessons were my sole companions. To be at school at the strike of the hour and to run back home as soon as the school closed, that was my daily habit. I literally ran back because I could not bear to talk to anybody. I was even afraid lest anyone should poke fun at me."

## ATTITUDE SHIFT

Gandhi struggled in high school. All subjects were taught in English, a language in which he was not yet fluent. Gandhi knew the mastery of English was critical if he was to become a successful politician. At the time, India was ruled by Great Britain as part of the British Empire.

At this time, Gandhi began to shape his sense of morality. A major influence came from the play *Harishchandra*, which he first saw when he was twelve. The play was about a king whose unfailing truthfulness and faithfulness to the gods costs him everything. His wife leaves him. His son dies. He loses his kingdom and becomes a slave. Finally, in the end, the gods restore all that the king has lost, rewarding his virtue.

According to Gandhi's autobiography, the play "captured my heart. I could never tire of seeing it. . . . 'Why should not all be truthful like Harishchandra?' was the question I asked myself day and night. To follow truth and to go through all the ordeals Harishchandra went through was the one ideal it inspired in me. . . . The thought of it all often made me weep."

# TURBULENT TEENS

At the age of thirteen, Gandhi was married to Kasturbai Kapadia. Neither he nor Kasturbai had any real say in the union. The custom in India was for parents to arrange marriages for their children.

At first, the marriage wreaked havoc on Gandhi's studies. Further complicating matters was that young Gandhi also had to tend to his father, who was ill. Kasturbai still spent much of her time with her own family, as was common with child marriages.

Life changed even more for Gandhi in 1885, when he was sixteen. That November his father died. And Kasturbai was pregnant with her first child. But the child died just a few days after its birth.

Two years later, Gandhi was ready for college. He chose a college he could

After graduating from high school, Gandhi *(right)* went to Samaldas College in Bhavnagar, India. In this photograph from 1886, he sits with his brother Laxmidas *(left)*, who also attended the college. Bhavnagar is about 186 miles (300 kilometers) from Gandhi's home town.

afford, Samaldas College in nearby Bhavnagar. But Gandhi was homesick there and confessed to having little interest in his studies. After a single term, he returned home.

# A TEST OF COURAGE

A family friend, who was a Brahmin (the highest Hindu social class), suggested that Gandhi go to England to study. Gandhi knew that a voyage to England—and life there—would be a test of his courage. He was still shy and timid, and those traits would not serve him well in a foreign country. But his mind was made up. "At that moment, my cowardice vanished before the desire to go to England, which completely possessed me," he later wrote.

In September 1888, eighteen-year-old Gandhi left his wife and new son, Harilal, to make the long voyage to England to study law at University College London. He had promised his mother that he would uphold his Hindu faith and would avoid meat, alcohol, and sex. But doing so was difficult. For example, Gandhi rented a room where meals were included. But the meals were prepared for meat eaters. In time, he found a good vegetarian restaurant as well as a book on vegetarian eating. Later, he was

Gandhi *(circled)* joined the Vegetarian Society while in London. As a vegetarian, he developed a strong belief that choosing not to eat meat is a moral choice as well as one that promotes physical health.

elected to the executive committee of the Vegetarian Society in London.

Gandhi prepared for the bar exam, the test that would make him a barrister, or lawyer. In 1891, three years after arriving in England, he accomplished his goal and passed the bar. It was time to return home.

# A DISAPPOINTING RETURN

Upon his return to India, Gandhi learned that his mother had died while he was away. The family had kept the news of her illness and death from him, wanting to spare him the pain while he was so far from home. Once home, Gandhi found it difficult to find work in Rajkot. He still battled shyness and in one instance couldn't bring himself to speak in court. He also struggled with his home life, where he was a terribly jealous husband. He later admitted that his poor treatment of Kasturbai in their early years was one of his great regrets.

Just as he was at a personal low point, an opportunity arose. His brother was friends with a Muslim who needed a barrister to handle a case for his firm, Dada Abdulla & Company. Gandhi was offered the job. There was just one catch: the job was in South Africa. Eager for a change, Gandhi jumped at the opportunity. Once again, he boarded a ship and left his family behind. (Kasturbai had given birth to another son, Manilal, in 1892.)

# A NEW PATH

In the 1890s, tens of thousands of Indians were in British- and Dutch-ruled South Africa. They were viewed as second-class citizens, much like black South Africans were. Twenty-four-year-old Gandhi came face-to-face with this reality right away. When he arrived at the port of Durban, he boarded a train for the city of Pretoria. With a first-class ticket in hand, he found his seat. At one stop, a white man came into the train carriage where Gandhi was sitting. The man looked at the brown-skinned Gandhi and immediately left to find railway officials.

The officials approached Gandhi and told him that he would have to move to the baggage carriage. First class was for whites only. Gandhi showed them his first-class ticket. The officials did not care. They insisted he move. Gandhi refused. The officials called the police, and Gandhi and his bags were physically removed from the train. He spent the night shivering outside the railroad station.

Gandhi had faced racial intolerance before. But something about this event sent him down a path that would change his life—and the lives of Indians—forever. Gandhi became immersed in the fight for Indian rights in South Africa. When his one-year contract with Dada Abdulla was finished in 1894, he chose to stay there. He helped to form the Natal Indian Congress, an organization devoted to improving the lives of Indians in South Africa. He returned briefly to India in 1896 and spoke out about the injustices faced by Indians in South Africa. After that, he took Kasturbai and his two sons back to South Africa with him.

While in South Africa, Gandhi *(top row, fourth from left)* helped found the Natal Indian Congress in 1894 to fight against laws that discriminated against Indians. Through efforts like this, Indians in South Africa became a unified political force for the first time in their history in South Africa.

# A VOICE FOR CHANGE

By this time, Gandhi's campaign for Indian rights had earned him some degree of fame in South Africa. He was a leader among the Indians there, but many whites saw him as a threat.

Meanwhile, the Gandhi family continued to grow. In 1897 another son, Ramdas, was born. Three years later, Kasturbai gave birth to a fourth son, Devdas.

In 1883 Gandhi married Kasturbai *(center)*, whom he lovingly called Ba. This photo of her with the couple's four sons *(left to right:* Harilal, Ramdas, Devdas, and Manilal) was taken in South Africa in 1902.

Gandhi's work in South Africa continued, but he constantly confronted resistance to change. In 1899 the British and the Dutch settlers (called Boers) were at war. Gandhi organized a group called the Indian Ambulance Corps and offered the British its medical services for injured soldiers. At first, the British refused this help. Only when the war escalated and the need for medical help became greater did the British relent. When the

British won the war in 1902, Gandhi and the ambulance corps had earned the grudging appreciation of the British.

Gandhi was relentless in his pursuit of Indian rights. In 1903 he moved to Johannesburg, South Africa, where he set up his own law office. He urged Indians to stand up against discriminatory laws. But he insisted that they do so nonviolently. He believed Indians should refuse to comply with unjust laws, a tactic called civil disobedience. He began by protesting against a 1906 law that required all Indians in South Africa to register with the government and carry a special certificate.

Gandhi and many other Indians refused to register. He was arrested and imprisoned for two months. Soon those who had registered for their certificates were burning them in public. More than two thousand Indians burned their registration cards at a mosque (Islamic house of worship) in Johannesburg on August 16, 1908.

Under Gandhi's leadership, Indians defied other unfair laws, including a ban on crossing from one South African state to another without government permission. Gandhi, his oldest son, Harilal, and many others received three-month prison sentences for breaking this law.

At the prospect of serving time in prison, some people would have turned away from their goals. But not Gandhi. Years later, he wrote: "The real road to happiness lies in going to jail and undergoing suffering and privations there in the interest of one's country and religion."

Gandhi continued the fight over the next several years. His law offices had become the headquarters for the resistance movement. He helped establish Tolstoy Farm (named after Russian author Leo Tolstoy), where families of people imprisoned for civil disobedience could live. He and his family moved to the Tolstoy Farm, and Gandhi took pride in making the bread for the farm. He also learned some carpentry and how to make his own clothing. A series of labor strikes and acts of civil disobedience eventually led to changes to many of the laws Gandhi and his supporters were protesting, including the registration law and a special tax on Indians.

It was far from total victory, but Gandhi felt his work in South Africa was done. It was time to return home to India.

# A NEW SPIN ON INDEPENDENCE

Gandhi famously made his own clothing. He had a hand-powered spinning wheel that he used to create cotton khaddar fabric. He would sit for hours, quietly working on his spinning wheel *(right)*. He believed that it was an important activity. By creating his own clothing, he was helping to free himself from dependence on British-imported fabrics. The spinning wheel would become an important symbol in the struggle for Indian independence. It even appeared on the Indian national flag from 1942 to 1947.

## A NEW MISSION

Forty-five-year-old Mohandas Gandhi and his family returned to India in January 1915. On his voyage back, Gandhi had made a decision to abandon the European-style dress he had adopted during his time in London. If he was to be a leader of the Indian people, he would dress in the traditional Indian style, covering himself in garments made of homespun cotton, called khaddar.

When Gandhi reached India, he got a hero's welcome. The Indian people were struggling to gain independence from British rule. Many wondered what role Gandhi would take in that fight. He decided to reconnect with his own people. So he traveled around India, meeting Indians and learning of their daily lives and struggles. At around this time, the Nobel-Prize-winning writer Rabindranath Tagore gave Gandhi the title Mahatma. As Gandhi traveled across India, crowds of people turned out to chant "Mahatmaji, Mahatmaji." (The *ji* suffix denotes respect and admiration.)

A united and independent India became Gandhi's new goal. However, unlike many nationalists, Gandhi was not just concerned with self-rule. He aimed for fair and proper self-rule. He pointed out that if done improperly, Indian self-rule could turn out to be worse than living under British rule. Gandhi had very specific ideas about how to accomplish independence. "If we act justly, India will be free sooner," he said. "You will see, too, that if we shun every Englishman as an enemy, home rule [independence] will be delayed. But if we are just to them, we shall receive their support."

After traveling the nation, Gandhi started an ashram (spiritual community or retreat) in western India. He lived in a simple house, declining the luxury that his fame could have afforded him. From his humble home, Gandhi set his mind to the question of Indian independence. He believed that India's own internal divisions were a weakness. Gandhi felt strongly that if Hindus and Muslims could overcome their long-standing hatred, the two groups could work together successfully to overturn British rule.

In 1917 Gandhi founded Sabarmati ashram, near Ahmedabad. Many years later, in the mid-1930s, he organized another ashram, which he called Sevagram (meaning "village for service"), in the town of Wardha. In this photo, he and Ba *(both seated on the porch of their hut)* speak to an assembly of young women at Sevagram.

The division created by the caste system only further divided the people. Gandhi wanted to reform this system too. In a controversial gesture, he invited a family of untouchables to live at his ashram. The ashram almost broke up because of the decision.

# BRINGING NONVIOLENT PROTEST HOME

Gandhi had used his ideas of nonviolence and civil disobedience to great effect in South Africa. He wanted to put them to work in India as well. He did so by helping indigo farmers stand up in 1917 to an unfair British system of payments. The next year, he organized a hartal (general strike) to protest a bill that would give the British government the right to put Indians in prison merely for suspecting them of being troublemakers.

When the hartal began, no Indians went to work or school. Shops closed and Indians gathered in prayer. Just as Gandhi had planned, the hartal began as a nonviolent affair. But it soon spun out of control. Violence escalated, and both Indians and British were killed. In one protest, a British general opened fire on protesters, killing hundreds and injuring many more.

In the end, the British realized that the furor caused by laws such as the Rowlatt Act (which gave the government powers to arrest people without warrants) would weaken their hold on India. The law was therefore voted down. But the damage was done. The violence that grew out of the protests marked a point of no return for many Indians. The nationalism movement had escalated, and both sides knew it.

Over the next few years, Gandhi's influence grew. He became one of the leaders of the Indian National Congress and the president of the All-India

"Nonviolence means courage of the highest order and therefore readiness to suffer. There should therefore be no yielding to bullying, bluff, or worse, even though it may mean the loss of a few precious lives."

—*Mohandas Gandhi, May 21, 1931*

Home Rule League. He worked hard to bring all Indians together for a common purpose. His eagerness to embrace the nation's Muslims as well as Hindus earned him respect from some and resentment from others.

Meanwhile, violence between India's Hindus and Muslims was on the rise. As talk of an independent India grew, Muslims feared a loss of representation in India, which they worried would eventually be ruled by the Hindu majority.

In 1924 Gandhi chose to fast (refuse to eat) until the violence ended. At first, this personal protest did little. But soon Gandhi's body grew weak. His followers begged him to eat, but he never wavered. The threat that the Mahatma could die became very real. Because he was revered by both Hindus and Muslims, the tactic worked. The fighting stopped. India was not ready to sacrifice its spiritual leader.

By 1929 India still had made little progress toward independence, so Gandhi organized his next major protest. This time, it was against a law that gave the British the exclusive right to gather and sell salt in India. Gandhi organized a march to the salt deposits on India's west coast. The twenty-four-day march in 1930 brought a trail of followers. Once at the coast, Gandhi gathered his own salt, in violation of the law. Gandhi's Salt March and the attention it gathered around the globe helped to put international pressure on Great Britain to give India more independence.

Gandhi picks up a handful of natural salt at Dandi, a town on the Arabian Sea and the final destination of his historic Salt March in 1930. During the 240-mile (386 km) journey on foot, Gandhi spoke to large crowds. By the end of his trek, tens of thousands of people had joined the peaceful protest march.

Gandhi's next effort was to organize a nationwide protest campaign called Quit India. Its demand was for the British to give up rule of India. The British knew how powerful Gandhi was as a leader of the masses. So before Gandhi was to give a major speech in 1942, they arrested him. When Kasturbai vowed to speak in her husband's place, they arrested her as well. Both were imprisoned.

The imprisonment was especially hard on Kasturbai, who was not in good health. She died on February 22, 1944, in her husband's arms. Gandhi was distraught. His own health began to decline. The British authorities released him from prison, not wanting the world-famous leader to die in prison.

# "A SPENT BULLET"

With Great Britain embroiled in World War II (1939–1945), India made strides toward independence. The British agreed to grant India its independence after the war. With self-rule on the horizon, the most pressing question was how India would govern itself. Would it remain united, or would it fracture into Hindu and Muslim states? Gandhi favored a united India, with all Indians treated as equals. But others disagreed—especially India's Muslim leaders. They wanted two separate nations—India for Hindus and Pakistan for Muslims.

By 1947 the two-nation solution had prevailed. Violence broke out as Hindus moved out of lands that would become Pakistan and Muslims moved out of Hindu-controlled India. An estimated five hundred thousand people died as a result of the violence. Gandhi was bitterly disappointed. "I have not convinced India [of my vision]," he said. "There is violence all around us. I am a spent bullet."

Even so, Gandhi continued to speak out in favor of peace and cooperation among all Indians. On January 12, 1948, he began a five-day fast, vowing not to eat until a greater unity among religious groups in India existed. This behavior enraged some Hindus, who believed that his sympathy for Muslims meant that he was turning his back on his own people.

Gandhi leads a public prayer meeting in New Delhi during his peace fast in January 1948. As in this photo, Gandhi often wore shawls that he had woven by hand.

Gandhi had always been controversial. Several attempts had been made on his life. But increasingly, more and more Indians—especially Hindus—saw his message of tolerance as dangerous. Gandhi knew that his life was in danger. Forces that stood against racial unity in India were preparing to move, and Gandhi was their target.

## Chapter Two

# TURBULENT INDIA

"Religions are different roads converging upon the same point. What does it matter that we take different roads so long as we reach the same goal?"

—*Mohandas Gandhi, n.d.*

To many, Mohandas Gandhi represented everything good about humanity. He stood for peace, tolerance, self-sacrifice, and unity. He fought oppression, not with guns or fists but with his mind and his heart. But not everyone viewed Gandhi this way. As he gained power and influence, some—mainly fellow Hindus—began to see him as a threat.

Why would Gandhi's message of peace and cooperation be viewed this way? To understand this point of view, which led to Gandhi's assassination, knowing something of India's history is key.

# DIVERSITY AND CONQUEST

India has been home to advanced civilization for more than forty-five hundred years. Its culture grew out of two main influences—the Indus Valley Civilization, which appeared around 2300 B.C., and the Aryans, who moved into the area around 1700 B.C.

Ancient India was a place of great religious diversity. As empires rose and fell and conquerors came and went, India's people were exposed to many faiths. By A.D. 320, Hinduism, with its many branches, was India's major faith. But foreign powers were bringing new faiths and ideas to India. Contact with the Roman Empire brought new ideas—including Christianity—and trade. Later, Islam, a faith founded in Arabia in the seventh century by the prophet Muhammad, reached India. Islamic conquerors had already taken over many of the lands west of India.

This figure of a carriage pulled by mules dates to the ancient site of Mohenjo Daro, one of the largest settlements of the Indus Valley Civilization. This civilization was centered in what are now Pakistan and northwestern India.

An unofficial truce existed between the Islamic conquerors and Hindu India for several hundred years. But to many powerful Muslims, Hindu beliefs were offensive. And the riches of India—gold and jewels—provided an almost irresistible temptation. The peace could never last.

In the early 1200s, an Islamic army under the Turkish commander Bakhtiar Khilji marched from central Asia into northern India. The Islamic fighters quickly conquered the Bengal region. From there, Khilji led his army into the heart of northern India and captured the city of Delhi. The Muslim invaders established the Delhi sultanate. (A sultan is similar to a king.)

Over the next five centuries, Muslim rulers and the native Hindus of India lived side by side. In some areas, such as Bengal and present-day Pakistan, Islam became the dominant religion. Hinduism held on through much of the rest of India, however. The Hindu population suffered greatly under Muslim rule. Hindus were killed by the millions. Their traditions and history were trampled. Hatred and distrust between Hindus and Muslims grew.

In spite of this, the two cultures influenced each other, creating a unique cultural blend. Some aspects of the Hindu caste system found their way into Muslim practice, as did stricter limitations on diet. In many circles, tolerance between the two faiths grew as converts to the Islamic faith recognized their Hindu countrymen as brothers, sisters, and cousins.

# THE MUGHAL EMPIRE

The strongest of the Islamic empires in India was the Mughal Empire. The Mughal Empire was founded in the early 1500s by Babur, a warrior and descendant of the famous Genghis Khan. The Mughal Empire ruled India for more than two hundred years.

# ENTER THE BRITISH

India had long been a desirable trading partner for Europe. Indian spices were a highly sought-after luxury in Europe. By the sixteenth century, Europe's interests and influence in India had grown. Europe became the driving force behind the next chapter in Indian history.

Throughout much of the sixteenth century, Portugal and Spain enjoyed a near monopoly on the Indian spice trade. Many Indians resented them, however. Portuguese missionaries had come with the traders' ships to convert India's people to Roman Catholicism. But in 1588, the British navy—with the help of a storm—defeated an armada of Spanish ships. The loss of the ships weakened the hold Portugal and Spain had on Indian trade. The Dutch and the British quickly filled the void.

In 1599 British merchants formed the East India Trading Company— later shortened to the East India Company. The company was formed to trade for Indian goods such as silk, tea, indigo dye, and the narcotic drug opium. The Dutch focused mainly on Indian spices.

At first, India welcomed the British. Unlike the Portuguese, the British made no attempts to convert Indians to Christianity. They even banned missionaries on their ships and at their forts.

In 1639 the British East India Company built Fort Saint George along the coast of the Bay of Bengal. It and the town that grew around it (Madras, later renamed Chennai) became a key trading port from which rice, cotton, and other goods were shipped from southern India to European markets. This engraving of the port dates to about 1860.

For the next one hundred years, the East India Company grew, remaining primarily a trade organization. Then, in the late 1600s and the early 1700s, India's ruling Mughal Empire fought several costly wars, and its power began to wane. The British saw opportunity. They brought growing military presence to India. Meanwhile, British agents worked to destabilize Indian leadership.

Soon the East India Company became more than just a trading company. When the British government uncovered corruption within the company, it took greater control of it. The company eventually became a part of the British government. It went on to rule large sections of India, complete with a military force and administrative offices.

Not all of India was happy with this takeover. A nawab (Muslim ruler) named Mir Jafar allied with the Dutch East India Company. Together, they launched an attack on the British. But it failed. Later, Mir Jafar's son-in-law, Mir Kasim, led another attack against the British along the Ganges River. The Battle of Buxar, as it was called, resulted in yet another British victory and further tightened British control of the region.

The British left the weakened Mughal Empire in charge as a puppet government. They set up a Western-style system of rule complete with tax and judicial systems. White Europeans were placed in high government positions. The British disbanded the Mughal army. It enlisted soldiers into the East India Company's military. Rebellion among India's people was met with swift and decisive military action. With these changes, India was under British control.

# DIVIDE AND CONQUER

As part of colonial rule in India, the British stripped Muslims of lands they had claimed for centuries and returned them to Hindus. Suddenly, Hindus had land, money, and relative social status. Muslims had little say in local government. Many of them were forced to work as landless farmers and laborers. In addition, the British set up separate elections for Hindu and Muslim voters.

# A CULTURAL MISUNDERSTANDING

In 1857 British officers issued new rifles to Bengal's sepoy army. The Enfield rifles used a special cartridge that was greased at one end. A soldier had to bite off the greased tip of the cartridge. Many sepoys (Indian soldiers) refused to obey the order to bite off the cartridge tips. The grease, it was rumored, was made of cow or pig fat. Putting cow or pig fat into their mouths was sacrilege, going against their religious beliefs. Many of the sepoys believed their Christian officers were using this order to deny them social status. Those who refused the order were stripped of military rank and sent home. This created an outrage among both Hindus and Muslims, leading to a bloody yearlong battle called the Sepoy Rebellion.

The British used the deep-seated mistrust between India's Hindus and Muslims as a way to control the people. The British deliberately drove a wedge between the groups. So long as Hindus and Muslims were in conflict, no united front could emerge to oppose British domination. The division played out at the highest levels of government. For example, high-ranking Hindus established the Indian National Congress in 1885 with the goal of promoting India's independence from Britain. The congress sought *svaraj* (self-rule) and had the backing of some British supporters. But Muslims in India led by Syed Ahmed Khan refused to join the Hindus in their efforts.

Syed Ahmed Khan was born in Delhi in 1817. He was a learned man and social activist, who helped form the All-India Muslim League in the early 1900s. The league favored the creation of Pakistan as a separate Muslim majority state.

Instead, Khan and Muslim political leadership decided that their interests would be best served by cooperating with the British.

Khan spoke about this position in 1888, foreshadowing future events:

> Suppose that all the English and the whole English army were to leave India, taking with them all their cannon and their splendid weapons and everything, then who would be the rulers of India? Is it possible under these circumstances two nations—the Mahomedans [Muslims] and the Hindus—could sit on the same throne and remain equal in power? Most certainly not. It is necessary that one of them should conquer the other. . . . Now suppose that the English are not in India and that one of the nations of India has conquered the other. . . . At once some other nation of Europe . . . will attack India. . . . Their governments are far worse, nay, beyond comparison worse, than the British government. It is therefore necessary that for the peace of India and for the progress of everything in India that the English government should remain for many years—in fact forever!

## GANDHI AND JINNAH EMERGE

When Gandhi returned to India in 1906, the Indian National Congress was quick to embrace the young barrister. Gandhi's ideas of love, tolerance, and nonviolence resonated with many Hindus. Gandhi increasingly became the voice for India's independence. He spoke out strongly against Western culture, claiming that the West's urban, technological society was a powerful force for evil. Great Britain and the rest of the modernized West was a soul-crushing machine, according to Gandhi.

While India's Hindu population embraced Gandhi as a leader, Mohammad Ali Jinnah became the voice of India's Muslims. Jinnah was the leader of the Muslim League, an organization founded in 1906 to protect the rights and interests of Muslims in India. Like many others in India, Jinnah also promoted Indian independence. He encouraged Hindus and Muslims to work together to meet that common goal. He later introduced his Two-Nation Theory, whereby an independent India would be split into Hindu and Muslim components.

While their approaches often differed, Jinnah and Gandhi shared the goal of expelling the British from India. And as anti-British sentiment grew in India,

Born in Karachi (Pakistan) in 1876, Mohammad Ali Jinnah (shown here in the 1890s) was a lawyer, politician, and the founder of Pakistan. He was the leader of the All-India Muslim League from 1913 until Pakistan's independence in 1947.

# SATYAGRAHA

In 1908 Gandhi came up with a new word, *satyagraha*, to describe his form of nonviolent resistance. The Sanskrit word means "insistence upon truth." He later described the movement:

Satyagraha differs from passive resistance as the North Pole from the South. The latter [passive resistance] has been conceived as a weapon for the weak and does not exclude the use of physical force or violence for the purpose of gaining one's end, whereas the former [satyagraha] has been conceived of as a weapon of the strongest, and excludes the use of violence in any shape or form.

Hindus and Muslims slowly began to come together. The Indian National Congress and the Muslim League formed an uneasy alliance. Jinnah and Gandhi agreed that change could only happen when Hindus and Muslims worked together toward a common cause.

# JALLIANWALA BAGH MASSACRE

The Indian nationalist movement took off in April 1919. In the context of protests against unpopular British wartime laws, British military office Reginald Dyer ordered his men, without provocation, to open fire on a large group of Hindus celebrating at a festival in Amritsar, a town in northwestern India. More than four hundred people died in what became known as the Jallianwala Bagh (Amritsar) massacre. Dyer was recalled to England and forced into retirement, but the damage was done. Many Indians who had been considered moderates in their

After the Amritsar massacre, General Dyer imposed martial law. As a form of punishment of Indian citizens, he also ordered public floggings (beatings with whips or rods), to which Indians in this photo from 1919 are being led.

approach to the drive for independence became convinced that more direct measures against the British were needed.

Gandhi continued to push for nonviolent action, including boycotts of British goods. But Jinnah and his followers favored direct action against the British. The Muslim League grew increasingly focused on open revolt, and the alliance between Hindus and Muslims began to fray.

# COUNTDOWN TO INDEPENDENCE

By the time of his famous 1930 Salt March, Gandhi had already emerged as a worldwide celebrity. His calm—almost mystical—manner endeared him to millions both at home and abroad. Across the world, he became a symbol of India's struggle for independence.

Just as the nationalist movement seemed to be gaining steam, however, the rift between India's Hindu and Muslim leadership was widening. The Indian National Congress insisted on ruling all of India. And with Hindus making up about 80 percent of all Indians, any representative government would be certain to be Hindu-dominated. Muslim leaders found this idea intolerable. The two sides were at an impasse, and no compromise to keep a united India seemed possible. Jinnah's Two-Nation Theory was looking more and more like a realistic option, which enraged extremist Hindu nationalist groups.

> "Non-cooperation with evil is as much a duty as cooperation with good."
> —Mohandas Gandhi, June 1, 1921

Still, the nationalist movement pressed on. In 1935 the British Parliament passed the Government of India Act. The legislation increased India's autonomy as a British province and set up a loose federal structure for India's government. Though the act left the British in charge, it marked a major step forward in India's quest for independence.

In 1939 World War II began. Great Britain and its allies went to war with Nazi Germany. Without consulting leaders in India, the British declared

India's entrance into the war. For many Indians, this was a grave insult and marked the time to force the issue of independence from British rule.

Jinnah took advantage of popular opinion. In 1940 he pressed the Muslim League to pass the Lahore Resolution, which called for India to be divided into independent Hindu and Muslim sections. The Hindu section would remain India, while the Muslim section would be Pakistan. Pakistan would include two disconnected regions—present-day Pakistan and Bengal, which would be known as East Pakistan.

World War II hastened the decline of Britain's global empire. By the end of the war in 1945, Britain knew it would be granting independence to most of its colonies, including India, in the near future. Hindu and Muslim leaders scrambled to find an acceptable compromise for postindependence India. The Indian National Congress opposed the idea of a separate Muslim-majority Pakistan, but Jinnah and the Muslim League would not be swayed.

In August 1946, tensions between Hindus and Muslims boiled over into violent civil war. Muslim refugees fled to the safety of the two halves of Pakistan, while Hindus living in those regions left their homes for India proper. Estimates vary widely, but hundreds of thousands—and perhaps more than one million—died in the chaos of the following year. Even after the worst of the violence was over, tensions remained high as the formal borders between the two new nations were negotiated.

In the midst of this violence and political turmoil, many Hindus gravitated toward a brand of extreme Hindu nationalism. Those who adopted such beliefs often leveled their harshest criticisms at Gandhi. They saw him as a traitor for his eagerness to work collaboratively with Muslims.

## GANDHI PLEADS FOR UNITY

Throughout the bloody civil war and the lengthy process of separating India and Pakistan into two independent nations, Gandhi begged both Hindus and Muslims to practice tolerance and nonviolence. He led prayers that combined Hindu, Muslim, and Christian readings. He condemned both Muslims and Hindus for atrocities committed against each other. He publicly supported Muslims suffering from persecution in Hindu-dominated areas.

In 1947, with the Indian Independence Act, India was finally free of British rule. The official day of independence was August 15. Yet extremist Hindu groups saw Gandhi as an embarrassment and as a source of national weakness. It was time, some extremists decided, for Mohandas Gandhi's influence—and his life—to end.

## Chapter Three

# THE TIPPING POINT

"The accumulating provocation of thirty-two years, culminating in his last pro-Muslim fast, at last goaded me to the conclusion that the existence of Gandhi should be brought to an end immediately."

—*Nathuram Godse, November 8, 1948*

Gandhi's position on relations between Hindus and Muslims in India infuriated many of his fellow Hindus. Despite a violent political climate, Gandhi never backed down from his message of peace and unity.

For decades the majority of Indians had embraced Gandhi's ideas and methods. But as the reality of Indian independence grew, many people openly disagreed with him. Among the most vocal were the followers of Vinayak Damodar Savarkar. An outspoken and controversial Hindu nationalist, Savarkar worked for a Hindu-controlled India. As a leader of the Hindu Mahasabha political party, he was one of Gandhi's harshest critics. He accused Gandhi of bowing to pressure from the British and from Muslim leadership in agreeing to the partition (splitting) of India and Pakistan. Hindu Mahasabha activists did not shy away from violence and were suspected of carrying out attacks of physical violence on Muslims.

By late 1947 and early 1948, the level of anti-Gandhi feeling was escalating. Members of Hindu nationalist groups traveled to Birla House (the location of Gandhi's public prayer meetings) in the city of New Delhi to question him directly during his prayer services. Others distributed pamphlets identifying Gandhi as pro-Muslim—a label that many saw as an insult. Some even threatened his life.

Threats on Gandhi's life were nothing new. Over the decades, several attempts to assassinate Gandhi had failed. But these new threats were different. They were no longer coming from a tiny minority of extremists. The issue of partition was forcing more and more Hindus to an extreme viewpoint regarding Hindu-Muslim relations. Gandhi's status as a revered leader diminished as well. Violence was in the air, and Gandhi was a visible, public target.

This was never clearer than on the night of August 31, 1947, in the city of Kolkata (Calcutta at the time). Gandhi was sleeping in his home there when a mob of angry Hindus broke windows and kicked in the doors of his house. The mob was carrying the body of a Hindu who had allegedly been stabbed by a Muslim. Gandhi quickly rose and tried to calm the crowd. But his words were drowned out by angry shouts. The police finally arrived and broke up the crowd with tear gas.

# HATCHING THE PLOT

When Gandhi announced on January 12, 1948, that he would begin a fast in Delhi in an effort to build unity between Hindus and Muslims, the news spread quickly. Media outlets, including a small newspaper called *Hindu Rashtra*, got the news over the teleprinter (an electronic typewriter that could receive and type messages from around the world). Based out of Pune in western India, Narayan Apte was the newspaper's manager. Nathuram Godse was its editor. The two were members of Hindu Mahasabha and followers of Hindu nationalist Vinayak Damodar Savarkar. Both had long held Gandhi's views in contempt. Like Savarkar, the two men believed that Gandhi's sympathies for the Muslim population weakened Hindus and India at large. They considered the partition of India to be intolerable. They went so far as to view Indian Independence Day, August 15, as a cause for mourning rather than celebration.

Gandhi, the Mahatma, could not be allowed to further weaken India. And there was only one way to silence him. Gandhi, they decided, had to die.

## MEET NATHURAM GODSE

At first glance, Godse was an unlikely assassin. He was an educated, literate, thirty-seven year-old newspaper editor. He was

"I embarked on the fast in the name of Truth, whose familiar name is God. . . . In the name of God we have indulged in lies, massacres of people, without caring whether they were innocent or guilty, men or women, children or infants. We have indulged in abductions, forcible conversions, and we have done all this shamelessly. I am not aware if anybody has done these things in the name of Truth. With that same name upon my lips I have broken the fast."

—Gandhi, January 18, 1948, two days before the first attempt on his life

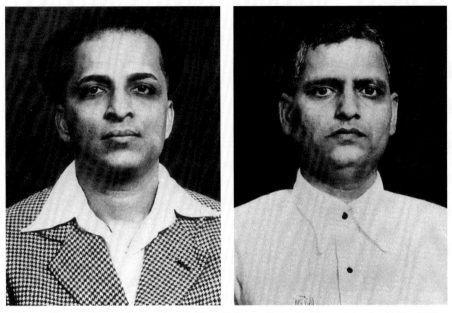

These police mug shots of Narayan Apte *(left)* and Nathuram Godse *(right)* were taken in mid-May 1948, shortly before the men went on trial for the assassination of Mohandas Gandhi.

born in Baramati in 1910 to a Brahmin family. They moved frequently during Godse's childhood. His father, an official with the postal service, was frequently transferred. Nathuram studied English in school but left school at sixteen and never finished his studies.

After several failed business ventures, Godse became obsessed with the Hindu nationalist movement. At twenty he joined the Hindu Mahasabha and read all the Indian history he could. As he learned more and more about his country's history under earlier Muslim empires and as part of the British Raj (empire), he became increasingly angry. He felt strongly that India was the birthright of Hindus.

Godse met a schoolteacher named Narayan Apte who shared his beliefs. Together, they started a newspaper called *Agrani*, which means "cutting edge." The name was later changed to *Hindu Rashtra* (Hindu Rule). Godse pulled no punches as he wrote editorials in the newspaper to speak out against Muslims in India, the British, and Gandhi.

One of the issues that most galled Godse was that of an Indian national language. Most Hindus supported Hindi as the nation's national language. But Hindi was not popular with many Muslims, most of whom spoke Urdu. So Gandhi backed an informal dialect called Hindustani—a cross between Hindi and Urdu. Godse saw this as a betrayal of India's Hindu majority population.

He commented, "Everybody knows that there is no language called Hindustani," Godse wrote. "It has no grammar; it has no vocabulary. It is a mere dialect, it is spoken but not written. It is a bastard tongue . . . and not even the Mahatma's sophistry [deception] could make it popular. . . . The charm and the purity of the Hindi language was to be prostituted to please the Muslims. All his experiments were at the expense of the Hindus."

Like Gandhi, Godse was devoted to the Hindu faith. But the two men had vastly different interpretations of how a Hindu should behave. Gandhi rejected all forms of violence. Godse, however, believed that the Bhagavad Gita, an ancient Hindu holy text, supported the use of violence to achieve a righteous goal.

Godse viewed the partition of India and Pakistan in 1947 as a massive failure, and he saw Gandhi as the man to blame for it. Making things even

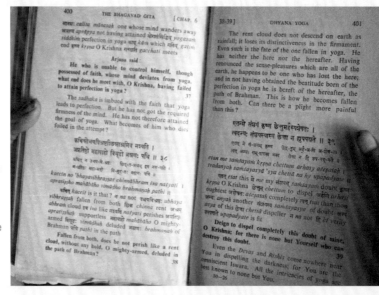

Godse turned to the Hindu text known as the Bhagavad Gita *(right)* to justify the use of violence. The seven hundred verses of the Gita involve a battlefield conversation between Prince Arjuna and his guide and charioteer Lord Krishna. They discuss a range of themes from the creation of the universe and devotion to God to the philosophy of yoga and self-realization.

worse in Godse's mind was that Gandhi had pushed for India to pay Pakistan a share of what had once been the assets of united India. Godse viewed this payment as an insult to Hindu power. In Godse's opinion, Gandhi had been corrupted by Islam and was a danger to the rights of Hindus everywhere. Godse could see only one way to fix this problem, and he was willing to be the man to carry out the solution.

## BROTHERS IN CONSPIRACY

History remembers Godse as the man who killed Gandhi, but he was not alone in his planning and execution of the crime. He had help from friends, family, and other like-minded people. Many have accused Savarkar of introducing the conspirators, but the connection has never been proven.

"Non-violence is not a principle at all. He [Gandhi] did not follow it. In politics you cannot follow non-violence. You cannot follow honesty. Every moment, you have to give a lie. Every moment you have to take a bullet in hand and kill someone. Why was [Gandhi] proved to be a hypocrite? Because he was in politics with his so-called principles. Is his non-violence followed anywhere? Not in the least. Nowhere."

—Gopal Godse, 2006, many years after Gandhi's assassination

Godse's main ally was his friend and colleague Narayan Apte. Apte was a former schoolteacher and a gun enthusiast. He had once started his own rifle club and had a good knowledge of firearms. In 1943 he served briefly in the Royal Indian Air Force but left after just a few months to care for his sick son. In 1944 Apte led a protest in the town of Panchgani against Gandhi's policies. In time, Apte became more and more absorbed in the extremist politics of Hindu Mahasabha. In Godse he found an ally and a trusted friend. Together they hatched the plot to kill Gandhi.

Godse's brother, Gopal, was another major player in the conspiracy. Gopal had once idolized Gandhi. But by the late 1940s, he had become an ardent Hindu nationalist like his brother. Unlike Nathuram, however,

Gopal was a family man. For this reason, Nathuram discouraged Gopal from playing too large a role in their plot.

## CO-CONSPIRATORS

Vishnu Karkare was a small businessman who joined the extreme Hindu nationalist movement in the 1940s. Karkare had lost both of his parents at a very young age and had grown up in an Indian orphanage. With little formal education, Karkare had taught himself to read. He established his own business—a tea shop that later expanded into a small hotel— in the city of Ahmednagar. Karkare's political views were deeply influenced by a 1946 relief mission to the Noakhali region of Bengal. This was the site of a massive slaughter of Hindus. While in

Gopal Godse, one of the conspirators in the Gandhi assassination, is shown here in a photo from 2003, two years before his death.

a Muslim-controlled region, he had witnessed atrocities committed by Muslims against Hindus, including the abduction of Hindu women. What he saw shook him and pushed him toward his extremist position. He joined Hindu Mahasabha, where he met Nathuram Godse and Apte.

Similarly influenced by experience was Madanlal Pahwa, a friend of Karkare. Pahwa was a young former member of the Indian Royal Army. He had spent time at a refugee camp in Mumbai (formerly Bombay) for Hindus displaced by partition. There, attitudes toward Gandhi and his political allies were sharply negative.

Minor members of the conspiracy included arms dealer Digambar Badge, who was involved mostly as a hired man. Shankar Kistayya, who worked for Badge, was also part of the group. Kistayya's role, however, was limited since he was mentally challenged and didn't know who Gandhi was. Kistayya didn't understand why he was to help kill him. Also accused as a conspirator was Dr. Dattatraya Parchure, the leader of a militant Hindu group called Hindu Rashtra Sena. The final member of the conspiracy, according to many, was Savarkar himself. Prosecutors were never able to prove his involvement, and it is unlikely he played an active role in the plot.

# PREPARATION

Once Godse decided to go through with the assassination attempt, he never looked back. Based on his actions leading up to the crime, it seems that he did not expect to survive the attempt. Some historians suggest he may have planned to take his own life once the deed was done. Once committed to the

This mug shot of Digambar Badge was taken in May 1948 shortly before the Gandhi assassination trial. He testified against the other conspirators and as a result was eventually pardoned and set free.

plan, Godse named the wives of Gopal and Apte as the beneficiaries of his life insurance policies. Godse was not a wealthy man, and his insurance policies did not add up to much. But he was determined that the families of his friend and his brother would get what little money he did have.

In the years after the assassination, many tried to paint Nathuram Godse as a madman. But his cold calculations and eagerness to take care of those who mattered to him paint a picture of a man passionate about the welfare of his people and his country. He was willing to do anything he felt was right—no matter how misguided his actions might have been.

In January 1948, Godse and Apte traveled to Mumbai. There they met with Savarkar—who may or may not have known of the plot at the time.

# VINAYAK DAMODAR SAVARKAR

The role of Vinayak Damodar Savarkar in Gandhi's assassination is still unclear. Some people claim that he masterminded the entire plot. Others insist that he knew nothing of it and was falsely accused because of his earlier dealings with Godse and Apte. Savarkar, born to a Brahmin family in 1883, got involved in the Indian nationalist movement while he was at universities in both India and England. He quickly became a revolutionary and started several nationalist youth groups. Through these groups, he advocated revolution against the British. This call to arms quickly got the attention of British authorities, who imprisoned him in 1910. Eleven years later, Savarkar agreed to give up his revolutionary ways. In return, he was released from prison.

Savarkar did not keep his promise. He remained a leader in the Hindu nationalist movement. Over the next two decades, he grew more and more frustrated with Gandhi's position of nonviolence. Savarkar believed open revolution was necessary and that Gandhi's stance was holding India back. He found like-minded individuals in the Hindu Mahasabha party and served as its president from 1937 until 1943.

By the late 1940s, Savarkar was one of Gandhi's most vocal critics. He criticized Gandhi for collaborating with Jinnah and India's Muslims, and he blamed Gandhi for allowing Pakistan to break away from India.

When Gandhi was killed in 1948, suspicion immediately fell upon Savarkar. Like him, Godse and Apte were members of Hindu Mahasabha, and both were associated with Savarkar. Additionally, Digambar Badge, who cooperated with the police investigation of the murder, had implicated Savarkar as a major player in the conspiracy.

When the conspirators were brought to trial in 1948, Savarkar defended himself vigorously in court. He was acquitted of all charges on lack of evidence. Public opinion was sharply against him, and angry Hindus pummeled his home with stones. Hindu Mahasabha faded into obscurity, taking with it any political power Savarkar had. In 1966, feeling his life had run its course, Savarkar renounced food, water, and medicine. He died on February 26, 1966.

At a January 14 meeting with the other conspirators, the details of a plan began to take shape. The initial plan was complicated and clumsy. Pahwa would throw a grenade during one of Gandhi's prayer services at Birla House. The explosion would cause mass panic, and in the confusion, the conspirators would be able to shoot and kill Gandhi.

# SETTING THE PLAN IN MOTION

The plan was in place, yet the group was poorly prepared. They had several grenades, guncotton (an explosive), and just two revolvers. One of the guns was owned by Gopal Godse from his time in the military, and a second was acquired by Badge from one of his clients in Mumbai.

Over the next few days, the conspirators traveled to New Delhi. Karkare and Pahwa arrived in the city first, on January 17, and checked into an inexpensive hotel. Karkare used a false name, but Pahwa checked in under his real name. Nathuram and Apte flew into the city later that day and checked into the Marina Hotel under false names. Badge and Kistayya were the last to reach the city, arriving by train on January 19. They stayed at the Hindu Mahasabha office there, and that location would become the command center of the operation. With everyone in place, the wheels were set in motion. The attack was set for January 20.

Early in the morning of January 20, Apte, Badge, and Kistayya drove to Birla House to familiarize themselves with the grounds and to walk through the plan. The others, including Nathuram Godse, who was suffering from a severe headache, stayed back. The three men entered the grounds to inspect the wooden platform upon which Gandhi would lead his prayers. There, they searched for the best shooting angles.

Satisfied that their plan would work, the conspirators returned to the Hindu Mahasabha office. There they inspected the two weapons they had for the job. Both guns were revolvers—small and most effective at close range. But both weapons were old and poorly maintained. The men took the guns to a wooded area to test them. First, they fired the weapon Badge had acquired at a nearby tree. But the shot fell short. The weapon was defective. The chamber of Gopal's weapon would not fire correctly either.

With just hours to spare, Gopal set himself to repairing the weapons. He had some knowledge of how they worked, likely from his time in the military. He was able to make what he thought were satisfactory repairs.

Meanwhile, the conspirators were tweaking their plan. The revised plan was for Pahwa to create a diversion by igniting a slab of guncotton during the prayer service, creating a loud explosion. Badge would be positioned behind a trellis near the platform. He would shoot Gandhi in the back during the confusion. Kistayya, armed with the other gun, would then fire at Gandhi from very close range. Once Gandhi was shot, the conspirators would all throw grenades to increase the confusion so the men could blend in with the crowd and escape without notice.

# A FAILED ATTEMPT

At around four thirty that afternoon, Nathuram Godse, Pahwa, and Karkare left for Birla House. The rest followed in a taxi about twenty minutes later. Everything seemed to be going according to plan. Karkare had arranged for Badge to get access to the area behind the trellis, saying that he would be taking photographs.

Things started to fall apart when Badge headed toward his position. A one-eyed man was sitting near the entrance to the room behind the trellis. This stopped Badge in his tracks. An ancient Hindu superstition says that a one-eyed man is bad luck. Badge was a superstitious man. He felt the appearance of the one-eyed man was a sign that the plot was doomed. So he took his gun and Kistayya's, left the Birla House garden, and tossed the weapons into the back of a taxi parked there. He was done with the plot.

Meanwhile, Pahwa ignited the guncotton to create the diversion that would signal the others to move toward Gandhi. The guncotton exploded as planned, but the conspirators didn't make their moves. No gunshots rang out. Nobody in the group threw any grenades. On the podium, a cool and collected Gandhi calmed the crowd. The assassination attempt had failed.

# BRUTAL INTERROGATION

**M**adanlal Pahwa *(right)* was interrogated and tortured as the police tried to learn about his co-conspirators. The police stripped Pahwa of his clothing and released biting red ants onto his naked body.

According to Pahwa, he did talk but told investigators mainly irrelevant details about the plot. He told them enough that they would believe he was trying to help them, but he intentionally threw them off the track that would have led to Godse and Apte.

The conspirators quickly fled the scene. All the men but Pahwa escaped. A young mother, Sulochana Devi, had seen Pahwa ignite the guncotton. She pointed at him to identify him for the police on the scene. The authorities arrested Pahwa. He later confessed to the plot and led police back to the Marina Hotel. There police recovered some letters and articles of clothing with Nathuram Godse's initials on them. But this was not enough to determine exactly who was involved in the plot.

The conspirators had failed in their attempt, but they had also learned from it. They would try again.

## Chapter Four

# ASSASSINATION

"Gandhi is being referred to as the Father of the Nation [of India]. But if that is so, he has failed in his paternal duty in as much as he has acted very treacherously to the nation by consenting to the partitioning of it. I stoutly maintain that Gandhi has failed in his duty. He has proved to be the Father of Pakistan."

—*Nathuram Godse, November 8, 1948*

The January 20, 1948, attempt on Gandhi's life had been a disaster for the conspirators. Pahwa was in police custody. Badge, put off by the poor execution of the first plan, left the group, refusing to have anything more to do with it. Kistayya left with him. The four remaining active members of the conspiracy—the Godse brothers, Apte, and Karkare—scattered.

Nathuram Godse realized that the initial plan had been too complicated. It had involved too many people and had too many ways to fail. He resolved to try again, this time by keeping things simple and relying on nobody but himself. He told Apte of his decision. "I am going to do it," Godse said. "I don't need any help, not another man. No recruiting of people, no depending on anyone else."

Time was of the essence, Godse knew. With Pahwa in custody, the police would be applying heavy pressure to force him to reveal the names of his conspirators. So on January 27, Godse and Apte traveled south to Gwalior, to the home of Dr. Dattatraya Parchure. Parchure provided a weapon, a 9mm Beretta revolver. From there Godse and Apte returned to New Delhi, where they reunited with Karkare and checked into a hotel under false names.

Godse was ready. There was no intricate plot, no diversions, no multiple shooters. He explained to Karkare why he would be acting alone. "Apte has responsibilities," Godse said. "He has a wife and child. I have no family. Moreover, I am an orator and a writer, and I shall be able to justify my act and impress the Government and the court of my good faith in killing Gandhi. Now Apte, on the other hand, is a man of the world. He can contact people and carry on the *Hindu Rashtra*. You, Karkare, must help in the conduct of the newspaper and carry on the work of the Hindu Mahasabha."

# JANUARY 30

Godse woke early on the morning of January 30. He bathed and dressed in a khaki jacket and blue trousers. He ate breakfast before taking his weapon into the woods to fire several test shots. The Beretta performed flawlessly. Godse engaged the gun's safety lock and tucked it away in his pocket.

# M1934 BERETTA

The weapon that killed Mohandas Gandhi was an M1934 9mm Beretta (the 1934 stands for the initial year of manufacture). The revolver, made in Italy, was first used as a standard firearm for the Italian armed forces. The M1934 Beretta is a semiautomatic, or self-loading, pistol. It fires bullets measuring 9 millimeters (0.4 inches) in diameter.

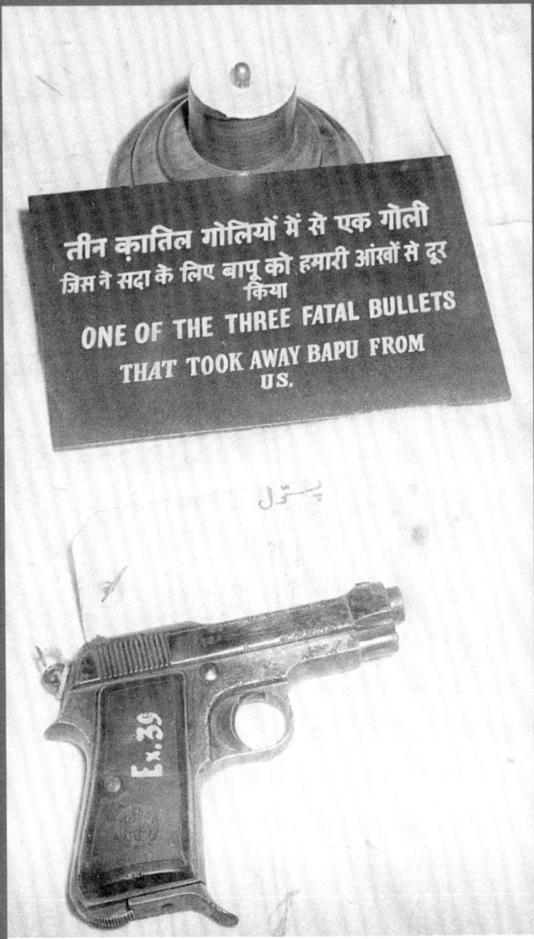

**M1934 SPECIFICATIONS**

**TYPE:** compact semiautomatic pistol

**TOTAL LENGTH:**
5.9 inches (15 centimeters)

**BARREL LENGTH:**
3.5 inches (8.8 cm)

**EMPTY WEIGHT:**
26.4 ounces (750 grams)

**CALIBER:** 9mm

**CAPACITY:** 7 rounds

तीन क़ातिल गोलियों में से एक गोली
जिस ने सदा के लिए बापू को हमारी आंखों से दूर किया
ONE OF THE THREE FATAL BULLETS
THAT TOOK AWAY BAPU FROM US.

Nathuram Godse used this revolver to shoot and kill Gandhi. One of the bullets fired from the gun is also shown at top. (*Bapu* is a Hindi word for "father" and in the photo above refers to Gandhi as the father of independent India.)

Godse sat alone on a bench in contemplation as Apte and Karkare traveled to Birla House. They returned about an hour later, reporting a heavy police presence outside the grounds.

At four thirty that afternoon, Godse left alone for Birla House. Apte and Karkare followed several minutes later. Despite the police presence, Godse entered the garden area without difficulty and made his way through the mass of people who had gathered for Gandhi's afternoon prayer meeting. Apte and Karkare later joined him, standing at his side. He either did not notice them there or chose not to acknowledge them.

Godse stood in silence. He waited.

## GANDHI'S FINAL MOMENTS

Gandhi, still weak from his most recent fast, had been through a turbulent week. At first, he did not realize that the explosion at Birla

Gandhi held regular evening prayer meetings on the grounds of Birla House in New Delhi. Hundreds of people attended the services, where prayers were read, hymns were sung, and Gandhi talked to spectators about his ideas and plans. He is pictured here (with grandnieces Manu and Abha seated in front) at the prayer meeting the day before his death.

House on January 20 had been part of an assassination attempt.

He said, "People have been sending me wires [messages] congratulating me [on my calm demeanor during the attempt] and praising me. In fact I deserve no congratulations. I displayed no bravery. I thought it [the explosion] was a part of army practice somewhere."

Yet Gandhi refused to allow the police inside his prayer meetings. The police could remain outside, he said, but he would not have uniformed officers at a prayer ceremony. In spite of this request, several plainclothes officers were inside the grounds on January 30. Gandhi discounted the idea that the police could protect him. "If I should die, I should like to die at the prayer meeting," he said. "You are wrong in believing that you [the police] can protect me from harm. God is my protector."

On the morning of January 30, Gandhi was up at three thirty in the morning. He said his morning prayers and then spent the next two hours working on a draft of a new Indian constitution for the newly independent nation. Finishing around six o'clock, he had a massage; a bath; and a meal of goat's milk, boiled vegetables, and orange juice. Then he took a short nap.

In the early afternoon, he listened as one of his helpers read the day's newspapers to him. He received several visitors. At about four o'clock, he returned to his room to prepare for the five o'clock prayer meeting. He ate another meal, then sat at his spinning wheel as he spoke with

Vallabhbhai Patel *(second from right)*, a leader of the Indian National Congress, helps Gandhi through a crowd of admirers in 1946. Both men worked passionately for India's independence, and Patel was at Birla House with Gandhi on the day the Mahatma was assassinated.

Vallabhbhai Patel, India's home minister (a cabinet member dealing with national security). They discussed a disagreement between Patel and India's prime minister Jawaharlal Nehru. The conversation stretched on past five o'clock, even though Gandhi loathed being late. Finally, Patel's daughter reminded the men that it was past five o'clock, and they agreed to meet with Nehru the next day.

Gandhi's grandnieces Manu and Abha helped him stand so he could head out to the prayer site. Gandhi was in good spirits. He joked with his grandnieces about the carrots they'd served him for his supper, calling it cattle fare. Several of his attendants, including Brij Krishna Chandiwala, followed behind Gandhi and his nieces.

Gandhi was close to his grandnieces Manu *(to his left)* and Abha *(to his right)*, with whom he walks in this photo taken in New Delhi in January 1948.

# THREE SHOTS FIRED

Manu and Abha helped Gandhi to the base of the stairs that led up to the prayer site. The large crowd that had gathered parted to let the Mahatma through. As was usual, people extended their arms, eager to touch Gandhi.

U.S. newspaper reporter Vincent Sheean watched as Gandhi approached the platform. He later described what he saw.

> We stood near the corner of the wall, on the side of the garden where [Gandhi] was coming, and watched the evening light fall on his shining dark-brown head. . . . It was one of those shining Delhi evenings, not at all warm but alight with the promise of spring. I felt well and happy and grateful to be here. Bob [Stimson, another reporter] and I stood idly talking, I do not remember about what, and watching the Mahatma advance toward us over the grass, leaning lightly on two of "the girls," with two or three other members of his "family" (family or followers) behind them. I read afterward that he had sandals on his feet but I did not see them. To me it looked as if he walked barefoot on the grass. It was not a warm evening and he was wrapped in homespun shawls. He passed by us on the other side and turned to ascend the four or five brick steps which led to the terrace or prayer-ground.

Nathuram Godse was looking at the very same scene. As Gandhi drew nearer to him, Godse sprang into action. He headed straight for the Mahatma and stood before him. Manu, believing that Godse simply wanted to touch Gandhi's feet (a common request of his followers), tried to brush him away. But Godse shoved her aside. According to some accounts, Gandhi and Godse exchanged words at this time. Godse later claimed that he had wished Gandhi well. Others deny that the two spoke at all. At 5:17 P.M., Godse reached into his pocket and gripped the 9mm Beretta. He pulled out the gun and fired off three quick shots. Two of the shots slammed into Gandhi's chest. The other one hit him in the stomach.

Gandhi's hands, which had been folded before him in a traditional greeting, slowly dropped. "*He Ram* [Oh God]," he gasped, then fell. (Gandhi's exact words here are a matter of debate. Some claim he said nothing at all.) Abha caught Gandhi as he fell, and the two slowly lowered to the ground, his head in her hands.

## THE AFTERMATH

The sound of gunfire and the sight of Mohandas Gandhi on the ground, a large red stain covering the front of his white clothing, set off mass confusion in the Birla House garden. Godse lifted his weapon and squeezed off a fourth shot. It presumably was meant for himself. A quick-thinking Royal Indian Air Force sergeant grabbed the gunman and wrestled the gun away.

A mob of people descended on Godse, beating him. Others in the crowd shouted "Kill him! Kill him!" The enraged air force sergeant was preparing to use the Beretta to shoot Godse, but the police prevented him from doing so. They arrested Godse and took him into custody. Apte and Karkare were able to blend into the crowd and flee to a train station, where they boarded a train bound for Mumbai.

As the drama surrounding Godse played out, Gandhi was rushed inside Birla House. His doctor was summoned. In his final moments, Gandhi was surrounded by many of his friends and followers as well as his grandnieces. Shortly after his doctor arrived, Gandhi, aged seventy-eight, was officially pronounced dead.

"For the present I only want to say that I am not at all sorry for what I have done. The rest I will explain in court."

—*Nathuram Godse, to a reporter shortly after his arrest, January 30, 1948*

## Chapter Five

# THE FALLOUT

"[Gandhi's] last journey has ended. But why should we grieve? Do we grieve for him or . . . for ourselves, for our own weaknesses, for the ill will in our hearts, for our conflicts with others? We have to remember that it was to remove all these that Mahatma Gandhi sacrificed his life."

—Prime Minister Jawaharlal Nehru at the scattering of Gandhi's ashes, February 12, 1948

The news of Gandhi's death spread quickly. Most Indians—Hindus and Muslims alike—were shocked and deeply saddened. In a few Hindu extremist strongholds, including Pune, his death was celebrated. Sweets were handed out in the street as was common when marking a festival. But the overwhelming national mood was one of sorrow and loss.

Prime Minister Nehru and Home Minister Patel addressed the Indian people by radio on the evening of January 30. "My heart is aching," Patel told the audience in Hindi. "What shall I say to you? My tongue is tied. This is a day of sorrow, shame, and agony for India. . . . The mad youth who killed him was wrong if he thought that thereby he was destroying his noble mission. Perhaps God wanted Gandhiji's mission to fulfill and prosper through his death."

Mohammad Ali Jinnah, by this time the leader of independent Pakistan, expressed similar regret. He had harsh words for any Muslim who had participated in violence against innocent Hindus. "Each one of us who has raised his hand against innocent men, women, and children, who has publicly or secretly entertained sympathy for such acts, is a collaborator in the murder of Mahatma Gandhi," Jinnah said.

## SAYING GOOD-BYE TO GANDHI

On the evening of January 30, Gandhi's body was displayed on a balcony outside Birla House for the masses of mourners to pay their respects. Gandhi was to be cremated and his ashes scattered in the city's Jumna River. The ceremony was delayed so that his son Ramdas, who was en route to New Delhi, could attend. Gandhi's son Manilal, who lived in South Africa, could not attend the cremation.

By the time Ramdas arrived late the next morning, a huge crowd of mourners had surrounded Birla House. The funeral procession included armored cars and a horse guard. A select force of marching guards from India's military moved alongside a carriage carrying Gandhi's body. The vehicle's engine remained off in recognition of Gandhi's rejection of some aspects of modern technology. The military guard physically pulled the

At Birla House, relatives and followers mourn at Gandhi's petal-covered body the evening of his death. His bared chest exposes the bullet wounds that killed him.

vehicle through the streets. Police lined the streets to keep the mourners at bay.

The procession moved at a snail's pace as thousands gathered to see Gandhi one last time. Hymns echoed through the streets. The procession to the banks of the Jumna River—a 6-mile (10 km) journey—took almost five hours. An estimated seven hundred thousand people, including major dignitaries from India and abroad, awaited its arrival.

At the cremation site stood a platform made of brick, stone, and earth. On top of this platform was a funeral pyre of logs, incense, and other materials. Gandhi's

"[Gandhi's] spirit looks upon us—nothing would displease him more than to see us indulge in violence. All our petty conflicts and difficulties must be ended in the face of this great disaster. . . . In his death he has reminded all of us of the big things in life."

—Jawaharlal Nehru, India's prime minister, January 30, 1948

body was set atop the pyre, and at quarter past four, his son Ramdas lit the pyre. The flames rose, and a chant of "Mahatma Gandhi has become immortal" rang out.

As the pyre burned, priests recited the Bhagavad Gita. The fire burned for fourteen hours. Then Hindu priests collected the ashes, which were given to the governors of each of India's provinces. From there, the ashes were to be thrown into a river or the sea. This way, Gandhi's remains would be spread all around the nation he had fought so hard to create.

The main ash-spreading ceremony was held on February 12, 1948, in Allahabad, where the Jumna and Saraswati rivers flow into the sacred Ganges River. Mourners packed the banks of the rivers. Gandhi's ashes

The day after the assassination and following traditional Hindu practice, Gandhi's body was cremated. The site of the cremation on the Jumna River in New Delhi is now a memorial known as Raj Ghat.

Crowds gather in Allahabad, India, for the final immersion of Gandhi's ashes in the sacred Ganges River on February 12, 1948.

were placed aboard a small craft carrying a group of friends and family. India said its final good-bye to Mohandas Gandhi as his ashes were poured into the water.

## CAPTURE AND TRIAL

Immediately after the assassination, Nathuram Godse was apprehended by police, but the other conspirators were able to slip away. Their escape would be short-lived. Badge was captured on January 31. Gopal Godse and Parchure were arrested on February 5. Kistayya was caught the following day. Apte and Karkare eluded the police for two weeks before they were finally caught in a Mumbai hotel on February 14.

The criminal investigation was thorough. Each of the conspirators was questioned extensively by police. Hundreds of others gave statements in the case.

Ultimately, Nathuram Godse and eight other men were charged with murder, conspiracy to commit murder, and other charges associated with the assassination. Justice Atma Charan presided over the trial, which began in Delhi on May 27, 1948, four months after the assassination. The court had decided that the case was too complicated and too emotionally charged to find an impartial jury of peers of the accused. In such a case, Indian law allowed for a trial in which a judge determines the verdicts. According to reports, Justice Charan was impartial and gave neither the prosecution nor the defense any cause to dispute the fairness of the trial.

Nathuram Godse went into the trial ready to proclaim that he had indeed killed Gandhi. He would argue that he had acted alone, without co-conspirators. He was willing to take all the blame to spare his friends.

Atma Charan *(top, far left)* was the judge at the trial of Nathuram Godse *(bottom right)*. The trial was held at the historic Red Fort, a fort and palace built by Mughal emperor Shah Jahan in the 1600s in Old Delhi (a historic part of Delhi, India's capital district).

Mounting a defense for Godse and the other men was a tall task. The official investigation had turned up the travel records of the conspirators. This was especially damaging to Apte, who had been at the assassin's side almost the entire time. In sworn testimony, Apte admitted to traveling to Gwalior with Godse but claimed that he had not returned to New Delhi. Likewise, Karkare denied being in New Delhi on the day of the assassination. Gopal Godse denied any connection to the conspiracy, as did Pahwa. (He claimed that he had set off the January 20 explosion as a measure of protest against the treatment of refugees.) Parchure, meanwhile, said that he was told he was helping in a peaceful demonstration. Savarkar denied any knowledge of the plot—a solid defense, considering the lack of hard evidence against him.

The weak spot in the defense was Badge and Kistayya. Badge was willing to cooperate with the investigation in hopes of receiving a lighter sentence. And the simple-minded Kistayya wilted under the pressure of courtroom examination.

Through it all, Nathuram Godse continued to proclaim that the crime was his and his alone. The trial stretched on for months. On November 8, 1948, Godse took the stand to make his statement before the court. It was the moment he had waited for. He had prepared thirty-three typed pages, which he read in English to the court. In his statement, Godse discussed his roots, his beliefs about Hinduism, and his duties to his faith. He explained how he came to believe Gandhi was a destructive force working against India's Hindus and why his act of assassination was one he considered to be for the good of all India.

"I took the final decision on the matter," Godse said before the judge. "But I did not speak to anyone whatsoever. I took courage in both my hands and I did fire the shots at Gandhiji on 30th January 1948, on the prayer grounds in Birla House. . . . I now stand before the court to accept the full share of my responsibility for what I have done and the judge would, of course, pass against me such orders of sentence as may be considered proper. But I would like to add that I do not desire any mercy to be shown to me, nor do I wish that anyone else should beg for mercy on my behalf."

Nine men were accused of plotting to assassinate Gandhi. They are *front row, left to right:* Nathuram Godse, Narayan Apte, and Vishnu Karkare. *Second row, left to right:* Digambar Badge, Madanlal Pahwa, and Gopal Godse. *Third row, left to right:* Shankar Kistayya, Vinayak Savarkar, and Dattatraya Parchure.

# JUDGMENT AND EXECUTION

Three months later, on February 10, 1949, the nine accused men gathered in the Delhi courtroom as the judgment was handed down. The judge found all but Savarkar guilty of at least some charges. Nathuram Godse and Narayan Apte were sentenced to death by hanging, while the others received prison time.

An appeal process immediately followed. During this time, the convicted men served their time in the Central Jail in Ambala, India (north of Delhi). Kistayya and Parchure won their appeals and were acquitted. The rest of the sentences were upheld.

Apte and Nathuram Godse were hanged in Ambala on November 15, 1949. As they walked to the single gallows upon which they would both hang, they shouted to the assembled crowd, "India united, may it be forever." Their hands were tied behind their backs, and black cloth bags were pulled over their heads. The men stood side by side as nooses were fitted around their necks. The order was given, and the chutes beneath their feet opened. Death from a broken neck was probably instantaneous. It did not go without notice that the hangings were an act of which Gandhi himself would have disapproved.

# POLITICAL FALLOUT

India's government wasted little time reacting—some claimed overreacting—to Gandhi's assassination. It moved immediately to ban Hindu extremist groups, including Rashtriya Swayamsevak Sangh (RSS), of which Godse had formerly been a member. Leaders of the RSS and Hindu Mahasabha were arrested. In cities around India, mobs gathered and burned Brahmin homes. (Godse and most other extremist Hindu nationalists belonged to the Brahmin caste.) Extreme Hindu nationalism, a movement that had been steadily growing, was all but abolished. Prime Minister Nehru, a close friend of Gandhi's, saw his weak control of the Congress strengthen. Patel remained as home minister, despite criticism that he had not done enough to protect Gandhi.

This is not to say that relations between India and Pakistan—or even internal issues in both countries—were without strain. India and Pakistan established diplomatic relations not long after the partition of 1947. Since then, the relationship between the two nations has ranged from strained to overtly hostile. While the issues dividing the nations have been many and complex, the core issue is a territorial dispute. Both nations have laid claim to the regions known as Junagadh and Kashmir, and decades of conflict and distrust have followed.

After Gandhi's death, Prime Minister Nehru—and later his daughter Indira Gandhi—led the nation's political left, which followed Gandhi's legacy of tolerance for all peoples. By the twenty-first century, new challenges were facing the nation, as the struggle between tradition and modernization raged. In Gandhi's time, he had taught about the dangers of technological modernization and strongly advocated for encouraging self-sufficiency, protecting local jobs, and maintaining ecological sustainability. But modern India has thoroughly embraced technology, and many see that as the key to India's future success.

# GANDHI'S GLOBAL LEGACY

In India Gandhi's birthday, October 2, is celebrated as a national holiday. His image appears on Indian currency. Many of the places where he worked and lived—and even Birla House (now known as Gandhi Smriti), where he was killed—have become shrines or museums. Millions of people visit them to pay homage to the man whom most Indians regard as a saint.

Gandhi's influence on the modern world cannot be overestimated. His actions and words still resonate for freedom-seeking peoples. He has served as the inspiration to countless movements. His teachings have been

A portrait of Mahatma Gandhi appears on the front of India's paper banknotes, including this five-rupee note.

# ON THE BIG SCREEN

In 1982 Columbia Pictures released the film *Gandhi*. The film focused on Gandhi's life, from his days in South Africa until his death. The film won eight Academy Awards, including Best Picture and Best Actor for Ben Kingsley *(below)*, who portrayed Gandhi.

credited with helping to overthrow dictators and to right injustices around the globc.

For example, Gandhi was a key inspirational figure for the young Martin Luther King Jr. King was a civil rights leader in the United States during a turbulent era of change in the 1960s. He was exposed to Gandhi's teachings at an early age and was influenced by Gandhi's stance

on nonviolence. King was so moved by Gandhi's ideas that he traveled to India in 1959 to meet with Gandhi's family and followers. "To other countries I may go as a tourist," King said of his trip to India. "But to India I come as a pilgrim. This is because India means to me Mahatma Gandhi, a truly great man of the age."

In many ways, the civil rights campaign that King helped to lead mirrored what Gandhi had done in South Africa and in India. King taught

U.S. civil rights leader Martin Luther King Jr. and his wife, Coretta (both draped with flower garlands), visited India in 1959. King was sometimes called the American Gandhi for his commitment to social change through nonviolent means.

# PRIZE MATERIAL

The government of India honors Gandhi by awarding the annual Mahatma Gandhi Peace Prize. Winners have included Nelson Mandela *(facing page)*, who led the modern fight for equality in South Africa, and Coretta Scott King, the wife of the late Martin Luther King Jr., for her continued efforts in the U.S. civil rights movement.

In 1999 *Time* magazine named its Person of the Century. Physicist Albert Einstein was ranked No. 1. Gandhi was ranked No. 2.

Protesters challenged racial discrimination at this Woolworth's store in Atlantic City, New Jersey, in 1960 through peaceful picketing. They were inspired by Martin Luther King Jr.'s insistence on nonviolent civil disobedience, which he modeled on Gandhi's methods.

civil disobedience and noncooperation with unfair segregation laws in the United States. He ordered peaceful sit-ins and marches and rejected all forms of violent protest. His movement was powerful and successful, though like Gandhi, King was shot and killed by an assassin, in April 1968.

Other dynamic leaders who were touched and changed by Gandhi's message include Nelson Mandela (South Africa's first black president), Tibet's Dalai Lama, Poland's Lech Walesa (a human rights activist), Cesar Chavez (a Mexican American civil rights activist), musician John Lennon, and U.S. president Barack Obama. Through their voices, Gandhi's powerful message lives on.

"Throughout my life, I have always looked to Mahatma Gandhi as an inspiration, because he embodies the kind of transformational change that can be made when ordinary people come together to do extraordinary things. That is why his portrait hangs in my Senate office: to remind me that real results will come not just from Washington——they will come from the people."

—President Barack Obama, then serving in the Illinois state senate, September 8, 2004

# SPEAKING TO TRAGEDY

**O**n January 30, 1948, Indian prime minister Jawaharlal Nehru addressed his nation, which had just learned of Gandhi's death. An excerpt from Nehru's powerful speech appears below. Can you find any other moving public tributes after other such tragedies? How are they similar? How do they differ?

Friends and comrades, the light has gone out of our lives and there is darkness everywhere. I do not know what to tell you and how to say it. Our beloved leader, Bapu as we called him, the father of the nation, is no more. Perhaps I am wrong to say that. Nevertheless, we will not see him again as we have seen him for these many years. We will not run to him for advice and seek solace from him, and that is a terrible blow, not to me only, but to millions and millions in this country. And it is a little difficult to soften the blow by any other advice that I or anyone else can give you.

The light has gone out, I said, and yet I was wrong. For the light that shone in this country was no ordinary light. The light that has illumined this country for these many years will illumine this country for many more years, and a thousand years later, that light will still be seen in this country, and the world will see it and it will give solace to innumerable hearts. For that light represented . . . the living, the eternal truths, reminding us of the right path, drawing us from error, taking this ancient country to freedom.

All this has happened when there was so much more for him to do. We could never think that he was unnecessary or that he had done his task. But now, particularly, when we are faced with so many difficulties, his not being with us is a blow most terrible to bear.

A madman has put an end to his life, for I can only call him mad who did it, and yet there has been enough of poison spread in this country during the past years and months, and this poison has had an effect on people's minds. We must face this poison, we must root out this poison, and we must face all the perils that encompass us, and face them not madly or badly, but rather in the way that our beloved teacher taught us to face them. The first thing to remember now is that no one of us dare misbehave because he is angry. We have to behave like strong and determined people, determined to face all the perils that surround us, determined to carry out the mandate that our great teacher and our great leader had given us, remembering always that if, as I believe, his spirit looks upon us and sees us, nothing would displease his soul so much as to see that we have indulged in any small behavior or any violence.

So we must not do that. But that does not mean that we should be weak, but rather that we should, in strength and in unity, face all the troubles that are in front of us. We must hold together, and all our petty troubles and difficulties and conflicts must be ended in the face of this great disaster. A great disaster is a symbol to us to remember all the big things of life and forget the small things, of which we have thought too much.

**1869**    Gandhi is born on October 2 in Porbandar, India.

**1883**    At the age of thirteen, Gandhi marries Kasturbai.

**1885**    The Indian National Congress forms to fight for Indian independence from British colonial rule.

**1888**    Gandhi travels to England to study at University College London.

**1891**    Gandhi passes the bar exam and returns to India and his family.

**1893**    Frustrated by a lack of professional progress, Gandhi accepts a one-year contract with Dada Abdulla & Company in South Africa. There he suffers discrimination and begins his campaign for Indian rights.

**1906**    Aga Khan and associates form the Muslim League to protect the rights of India's Muslim population.

**1908**    Gandhi coins the term *satyagraha*, which means "insistence upon truth."

**1910**    Nathuram Godse is born on May 19 in Baramati, India.

**1915**    Gandhi returns to India and begins a tour of his homeland.

**1924**    Gandhi is released from prison due to an attack of appendicitis.

**1930**    Gandhi leads the Salt March to the Arabian Sea to protest British taxation of salt.

**1931**    Gandhi travels to England to attend a conference on the future of India.

| 1935 | The British pass the Government of India Act of 1935, increasing India's autonomy and paving the way for independence. |
|---|---|
| 1944 | Kasturbai dies in Gandhi's arms. |
| 1946 | Violence between Hindus and Muslims breaks out as India and Pakistan prepare for partition and self-rule. |
| 1947 | Britain formally relinquishes control of India, and India and Pakistan become independent nations. |
| 1948 | On January 12, Gandhi announces his plan to begin a fast in New Delhi in an effort to unify Hindus and Muslims. Nathuram Godse and Narayan Apte make plans to assassinate him. |
| | Godse and Apte fly to New Delhi under false names on January 17. |
| | Godse, Apte, and their co-conspirators make a failed attempt to assassinate Gandhi on January 20. |
| | On January 27, Godse and Apte return to New Delhi. |
| | Godse shoots Gandhi three times before an afternoon prayer meeting at Birla House on January 30. Gandhi dies from his wounds. Godse is arrested. |
| | Gandhi is cremated and his ashes are scattered in the Jumna River on January 31. |
| | The trial of Godse and his co-conspirators begins on May 27. |
| 1949 | Godse and Apte are found guilty and are hanged in Ambala on November 15. |

# WHO'S WHO?

**NARAYAN DATTATRAYA APTE (1911–1949)** Apte was the main conspirator with Nathuram Godse. Little is known about his early life, but he graduated from Bombay University in 1932. He took a teaching job after graduating. In 1939 he joined Hindu Mahasabha. Through this group, he met Nathuram Godse. The two worked together on a small newspaper, and Apte served as its manager. In January 1948, the two men hatched a plot to kill Gandhi, a political adversary. Their first attempt failed, but the second, which occurred on January 30, succeeded. Apte was standing at Godse's side until the shots were fired. Apte eluded capture for two weeks before being arrested in Mumbai. He was tried and found guilty of murder in 1949. For the crime, he was hanged in November 1949.

**HARILAL GANDHI (1888–1948)** Mohandas Gandhi's eldest son, Harilal, was born in Rajkot, India, though most of his childhood was spent in South Africa. Harilal dreamed of being like his father. He wanted to travel to London to be educated as a lawyer. His father would not support him, feeling that a Western education would not be helpful. Harilal rebelled at this treatment, cutting off ties with his family. He briefly converted to Islam and took on the name Abdullah Gandhi, though in time he returned to Hinduism. This did not bother his father, though his alleged alcoholism and criminal behavior did. Harilal went to Delhi for his father's funeral in 1948, but virtually no one recognized him. He died later that year from liver disease, likely a result of a lifetime of heavy drinking.

**KASTURBAI GANDHI (1869–1944)** Born in Gujarat, India, Kasturbai married Mohandas Gandhi at the age of fourteen. She bore five children, though only four sons survived infancy. Kasturbai shared the Mahatma's positions and frequently took his place at protests and speeches when he was in prison for his civil disobedience campaigns. Several times she was imprisoned for her actions. She died in prison in 1944, after having been incarcerated in 1942 for speaking out against the British.

**MANILAL GANDHI (1892–1956)** Gandhi's second son was born in South Africa. From an early age, he was active in his father's political campaigns. Like most of his family, he served several prison terms for his civil disobedience. Beginning in 1917, Manilal served as the editor of the *Indian Opinion*, which had been established by his father to help spread the word about the fight for Indian independence. Manilal married and had three children. He died of a stroke in 1956.

**NATHURAM VINAYAK GODSE (1910–1949)** The assassin of Mohandas Gandhi was born in Baramati, India, to a Brahmin family. As a child, Godse idolized Gandhi. But his devotion didn't last long. By the age of twenty, Godse had joined Hindu Mahasabha, a nationalist organization, and considered Gandhi a political enemy. He served as the editor of a small newspaper, promoting the virtues of the Hindu nationalist movement. He often sharply criticized Gandhi's policies, which he felt weakened Hindu India. In January 1948, he decided that Gandhi had to be eliminated. He led a failed assassination attempt on January 20, then succeeded in shooting and killing the Mahatma on January 30. Godse was tried and found guilty of murder in 1949. For the crime, he was hanged in November 1949.

**MOHAMMAD ALI JINNAH (1876–1948)** Jinnah, whose place and even year of birth are a matter of dispute, was called by many the Father of Pakistan. Like Gandhi, Jinnah spent time studying law in London, England. When he returned to India, he became increasingly involved in politics. In 1896 he became a member of the Indian National Congress. In time, he joined the Muslim League and became its president in 1916. Gandhi and Jinnah were, at different times, political allies and adversaries. Jinnah's Two Nations theory eventually led to the partition of India, and he was Pakistan's first governor-general. He died in September 1948 of complications from tuberculosis.

**VISHNU RAMAKRISHNA KARKARE (1910–1974)** Karkare was one of the three conspirators at Birla House on the day of Gandhi's assassination. As an orphan, his date and place of birth were unknown even to him. He had little formal schooling, though he taught himself to read. At around the age of fifteen, Karkare started his own tea shop in Ahmednagar and later expanded it into a small hotel. In 1946 or 1947, he traveled on a relief mission into a region of India torn by violence between Hindus and Muslims. The violence he witnessed there (mainly Muslim violence against Hindus) deeply changed him, pushing him toward an extreme Hindu nationalism. He connected with Godse and Apte and joined the conspiracy to kill Gandhi. He was arrested shortly after the crime and remained in prison until 1964. He died ten years later of a heart attack.

**JAWAHARLAL NEHRU (1889–1964)** Born in Allahabad, India, Nehru was India's first and longest-serving prime minister. The son of a wealthy Hindu lawyer, Nehru seemed born to lead. At a young age, he rose to a leadership position among the liberal wing of the Indian National Congress. Gandhi was a mentor to young Nehru, and this relationship helped Nehru become elected India's first prime minister. He held that office until his death from a heart attack in 1964.

**SARDAR VALLABHBHAI PATEL (1875–1950)** Born in Nadiad, India, to a family of modest means, Patel was a self-made man. He worked to put himself through school—going so far as to borrow books from classmates to save the expense of buying them—and become a lawyer. After the death of his young wife from cancer, Patel grew absorbed in the Indian nationalist movement. He was a follower of Gandhi's, campaigning for the Mahatma's campaigns of civil disobedience and nonviolence. Upon independence, Patel became the nation's first home minister and deputy prime minister. He died in 1950 of a heart attack. *Sardar* is an honorary title attached to Patel's name, meaning "chief."

**RABINDRANATH TAGORE (1861–1941)** Considered by most to be the greatest writer in Indian history, Tagore was born in Kolkata, India, to a wealthy Brahmin family. He was writing poetry by the age of eight. Later, he wrote fiction and drama, and composed music. He moved away from classical forms of art and literature to write more modern poetry and fiction, and it earned him the Nobel Prize for Literature in 1913. Tagore was an Indian nationalist and embraced Mohandas Gandhi as a friend and ally. It was Tagore who conferred upon Gandhi the title Mahatma.

# GLOSSARY

**ASHRAM:** a religious or spiritual retreat

**CASTE:** a class of Hindu society. Most Hindus are born into one of four major classes, Brahmin, Kshatriya, Vaishya, and Sudra.

**CIVIL DISOBEDIENCE:** the act of nonviolently defying unjust laws

**CONSPIRACY:** a secret plot between two or more people to commit an illegal act

**HARTAL:** a general strike, in which a large group of people refuse to do their normal daily activities, such as going to work or school

**KHADDAR:** a type of homespun cotton fabric that Gandhi made and used for his own clothing

**MAHATMA:** a title meaning "great soul"

**SATYAGRAHA:** a Sanskrit word, meaning "insistence upon truth," that Gandhi coined to describe his form of nonviolent resistance

**SEPOY:** an Indian who served in the British Army during the era of British colonial rule

**UNTOUCHABLE:** an Indian citizen born outside of the caste system. Untouchables, known in modern times as Dalit, were historically considered the lowest level of society and performed the least desirable jobs. Their social position has improved in modern times, but they still face prejudice in parts of India.

# SOURCE NOTES

4 Robert Trumbull, "Gandhi Is Killed by a Hindu; India Shaken, World Mourns; 15 Die in Rioting in Bombay," *New York Times*, January 31, 1948.

5 Ibid.

6 Richard Attenborough, *The Words of Gandhi* (New York: Newmarket Press, 2000), 12.

9 Mohandas Gandhi, *Autobiography: The Story of My Experiments with Truth* (New York: Dover Publications, 1983), 4.

10 Ibid., 5.

11 Ibid., 33.

15 Louis Fischer, *Gandhi: His Life and Messages for the World* (New York: Mentor, 1982), 38.

17 Ibid., 52.

18 Attenborough, *The Words of Gandhi*, 53–54.

20 Fischer, *Gandhi: His Life and Messages for the World*, 155.

22 Attenborough, *The Words of Gandhi*, 63.

28 Stanley Wolpert, *India* (Berkeley: University of California Press, 2005), 59–60.

29 *New York Times*, "Millions Esteemed Gandhi as a Saint," January 31, 1948.

31 Attenborough, *The Words of Gandhi*, 53–54.

34 Yogesh Chadha, *Gandhi: A Life* (New York: John Wiley & Sons, 1997), 498.

36 Homer A. Jack, ed. *The Gandhi Reader: A Sourcebook of His Life and Writings* (New York: Grove Press, 2002), 463.

38 Chadha, *Gandhi: A Life*, 499.

39 *Time Magazine*, "His Principle of Peace Was Bogus," February 14, 2000, http://www.time.com/time/world/article/0,8599,2055031,00.html (December 12, 2012).

46 Chanda, *Gandhi: A Life*, 500.

47 Ibid., 499.

47 Ibid., 492.

50 Rajmohan Gandhi, *Gandhi: The Man, His People, and the Empire* (Berkeley: University of California Press, 2007), 648–649.

50 Chadha, *Gandhi: A Life*, 461.

52 Ibis Communications, "The Assassination of Gandhi, 1948," *EyeWitness to History*, n.d., http://www.eyewitnesstohistory.com/gandhi.htm (November 28, 2012).

53 Richard L. Johnson, *Gandhi's Experiments with Truth: Essential Writings by and about Mahatma Gandhi* (Lanham, MD: Lexington Books, 2006), 49.

53 Chadha, *Gandhi: A Life*, 493.

53 Ibid., 486.

54 Stanley Wolpert, *Gandhi's Passion: The Life and Legacy of Mahatma Gandhi* (Oxford: Oxford University press, 2001), 259.

55 Rajmohan Gandhi, *Gandhi*, 658.

55 Ibid., 657.

56 Trumbull, "Gandhi Is Killed by a Hindu."

57 Margaret Parton, "Gandhi's Ashes Mixed with Holy Waters as Millions Look On," *Pittsburgh Post-Gazette*, February 13, 1948, http://news.google.com/newspapers?nid=1129&dat=19480213&id=iuYMAAAAIBAJ&sjid=hmoDAAAAIBAJ&pg=2065,2460132 (Deember 12, 2012).

60 Rajmohan Gandhi, *Gandhi*, 500–501.

61 Ibid., 502.

65 Wolpert, *Gandhi's Passion*, 264.

67 *Hindu*, "Obama Reluctant to Seek Changes in Nuclear Deal," December 7, 2008, http://www.hinduonnet.com/thehindu/thscrip/print.pl?file=2008071260521800.htm&date=2008/07/12/&prd=th& (December 12, 2012).

# SELECTED BIBLIOGRAPHY

Attenborough, Richard. *The Words of Gandhi*. New York: Newmarket Press, 2000.

Chadha, Yogesh. *Gandhi: A Life*. New York: John Wiley & Sons, 1997.

Easwaran, Eknath. *Gandhi, the Man: The Story of His Transformation*. Tomales, CA: Nilgiri Press, 1997.

Fischer, Louis. *Gandhi: His Life and Messages for the World*. New York: Mentor, 1982.

Gandhi, Mohandas. *Autobiography: The Story of My Experiments with Truth*. New York: Dover Publications, 1983.

Gandhi, Rajmohan. *Gandhi: The Man, His People, and the Empire*. Berkeley: University of California Press, 2007.

Keay, John. *India: A History*. New York: Atlantic Monthly Press, 2000.

*New York Times*, "Millions Esteemed Gandhi as a Saint," January 31, 1948.

Trumbull, Robert. "Gandhi Is Killed by a Hindu; India Shaken, World Mourns; 15 Die in Rioting in Bombay." *New York Times*, January 31, 1948.

Wolpert, Stanley. *Gandhi's Passion: The Life and Legacy of Mahatma Gandhi*. Oxford: Oxford University Press, 2001.

———. *India*. Berkeley: University of California Press, 2005.

# FOR FURTHER INFORMATION

Corrick, James A. *Ancient India*. San Diego: Lucent Books, 2005.
  Read more about ancient India, its people, culture, and legacy. Corrick details the major empires that ruled the Indian subcontinent and explains the role of religion played in its development.

Crompton, Samuel Willard. *Nelson Mandela: Ending Apartheid in South Africa*. New York: Chelsea House, 2007.
  This biography details the life and struggles of South Africa's Nelson Mandela, a man whose methods to end Apartheid in South Africa were influenced by Gandhi.

Darby, Jean. *Martin Luther King Jr.* Minneapolis: Lerner Publications, 2005.
  Learn about U.S. civil rights leader Martin Luther King Jr. in this biography. King was deeply influenced by Gandhi and adopted his stance on nonviolent protest.

Downing, David. *Mohandas Gandhi*. Chicago: Heinemann Library, 2002.
  This short biography touches on the highlights of Gandhi's life, including his use of nonviolent protest in his quest for Indian independence.

Engfer, Lee. *India in Pictures*. Minneapolis: Twenty-First Century Books, 2003.
  This title, a part of the popular Visual Geography Series, investigates India's history, culture, major religions, topography, and much more.

*Gandhi*. DVD. Directed by Richard Attenborough. Culver City, CA: Columbia TriStar Home Video, 2001.
  This Academy-Award-winning film depicts Gandhi, from his time in South Africa until his death.

*Google News: India*
  http://news.google.co.in/
  For the latest news about India, check out Google News. It includes links to a wide variety of stories dealing with India, from politics to entertainment and sports.

Hamilton, Janice. *South Africa in Pictures*. Minneapolis: Twenty-First Century Books, 2004.
  Learn about the country where Gandhi first made his mark as a leader for human rights. This title includes a wide range of information about South Africa, including its history, people, and geography.

*Hindu*

http://www.hinduonnet.com/

The online edition of India's national newspaper, the *Hindu*, includes material from the print edition, as well as the special Web content.

*Hinduism Today*

http://www.hinduismtoday.com

To read more about Hinduism in the present day, check out the online version of *Hinduism Today*. The site includes an introduction to the faith, answers frequently asked questions, and links to a range of news stories on Hinduism.

"India: Pinch of Salt"

http://www.time.com/time/magazine/article/0,9171,738958,00.html

Read this article, originally published in *Time* in 1930, about Gandhi's Salt March and its impact on India's quest for independence.

Kuhn, Betsy. *The Force Born of Truth*. Minneapolis: Twenty-First Century Books, 2011.

This is the story of Gandhi's struggle for the rights of the Indian people focusing on his Salt March in 1930.

*MKGandhi*

http://www.mkgandhi.org

MKGandhi.org is the place to go on the Web to read more about Gandhi's fascinating life. The site includes sections on Gandhi's writings, philosophy, exercises in nonviolence, and much more.

*News: International*

http://www.thenews.com.pk

The online, international version of Pakistan's number one English-language newspaper contains all the latest news coming out of Pakistan.

*New York Times on the Web*

http://www.nytimes.com

This online version of the newspaper offers current news stories along with an archive of articles on India.

Nicholson, Michael. *Mahatma Gandhi: A Leader of Indian Independence*. San Diego: Blackbirch Press, 2003.

Nicholson explores Gandhi, his life and mission, and his role in securing Indian independence from Great Britain.

Taus-Bolstad, Stacy. *Pakistan in Pictures*. Minneapolis: Twenty-First Century Books, 2003.

This title, a part of the popular Visual Geography Series, investigates Pakistan's history, including its split from India, as well as its people, geography, and much more.

*Times of India*

http://timesofindia.indiatimes.com

The website of this newspaper is a great source of current news on India. The site includes editorials, polls, and a world perspective.

Todd, Anne M. *Mohandas Gandhi*. Philadelphia: Chelsea House, 2004.

The author details Gandhi's life, focusing on his major political achievements and the steps he took to help India gain independence from Great Britain.

Wangu, Madhu Bazaz. *Hinduism*. New York: Chelsea House, 2009.

Learn more about Hinduism—Gandhi's religion—its origins, principles, and place in the modern world.

# INDEX

# PHOTO ACKNOWLEDGMENTS

The images in this book are used with the permission of: © Dinodia Photos/Hulton Archive/Getty Images, p. 4; © Dinodia Photos/Alamy, pp. 7 (both), 10, 11, 13, 14, 17, 19, 49, 51, 58; © Miller/Topical Press Agency/Hulton Archive/Getty Images, p. 16; AP Photo, pp. 21, 48, 50, 56, 66; Alfredo Dagli Orti/ The Art Archive at Art Resource, NY, p. 23; © Universal Images Group/Getty Images, p. 25; Wikimedia Commons, p. 27; © Bettmann/CORBIS, p. 29; © TopFoto/The Image Works, p. 30; © Mondadori/Getty Images, pp. 37 (both), 41, 45; © Louise Batalla Duran/Alamy, p. 38; AP Photo/Tim Sullivan, p. 40; © Sunil Malhotra/Alamy, p. 57; © Fox Photos/Hulton Archive/Getty Images, p. 59; © Topham/The Image Works, p. 61; © age fotostock/SuperStock, p. 63; © Columbia Pictures/Courtesy Everett Collection, p. 64; AP Photo/R. Satakopan, p. 65; AP Photo/John Parkin, p. 67.

Front cover: © Fox Photos/Hulton Archive/Getty Images.

Main body text set in Gamma ITC Std Book 11/15. Typeface provided by International Typeface Corp.

# AUTHOR BIOGRAPHY

Matt Doeden is a freelance writer and editor who has written or edited hundreds of books on a wide range of topics. His interest in Gandhi was piqued after seeing the award-winning 1982 film, *Gandhi*, and he jumped at the chance to research and write a book about this fascinating man and the men who conspired to take his life. Doeden lives in Minnesota with his wife and two children.